Duets for Bear Lovers

Elementary Duets for 1 Piano, 4 Paws

Margaret Goldston

FOREWORD

In this collection of duets the primo and secondo parts are EQUAL IN DIFFICULTY. Hand positions for the beginning of each piece are shown; however, easy position changes occur within some of the pieces.

Teachers and students alike will be richly rewarded with the benefits derived from duets. Practicing piano can be a lonely experience, but the "work" becomes "play" when sharing it with someone else. Duets help pupils learn to keep a steady rhythm and achieve continuity in their performance. Also, duets add variety to the lesson plan or recital program. Teachers of group lessons use duets as an indispensable part of their class activities.

In addition to group classes, the two parts can be assigned to a sister and brother, child and parent, neighbors, or students with lessons scheduled consecutively without arranging extra practices. I made the discovery that many parents of my students had in the past studied piano sufficiently to be able to play the easy second part. The shared family activity resulted in increased parental interest and support.

My students who tried the duets were in their first year of piano study, between the last quarter of their first book extending through the second book. Contributing to our success was the fact that we combined the parts only AFTER mastering them separately and then with a very slow tempo and counting aloud. So enthusiastic were the students about *Duets for Bear Lovers* that I had a delightful time teaching them! I hope you have a similar experience.

CONTENTS

D1399228

Bears on Wheels

(Performed by the Cub Club)

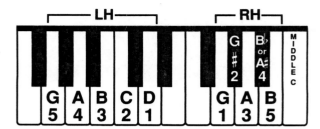

Playfully

Bears on Wheels

(Performed by the Cub Club)

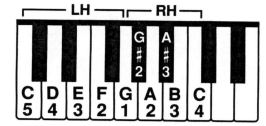

Playfully

Both hands 8va higher throughout* 1

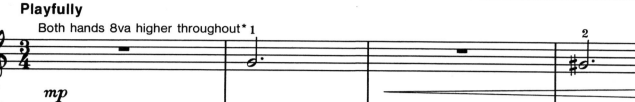

* It is also possible to play this piece as written instead of 8va higher.

Bears on Wheels

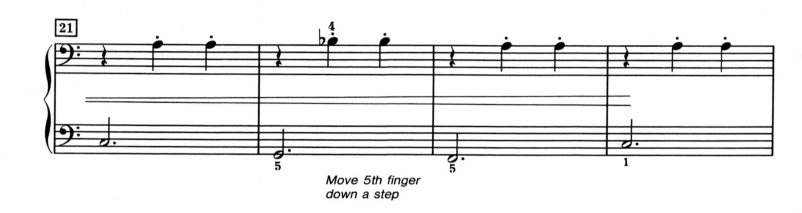

Move 5th finger
down a step

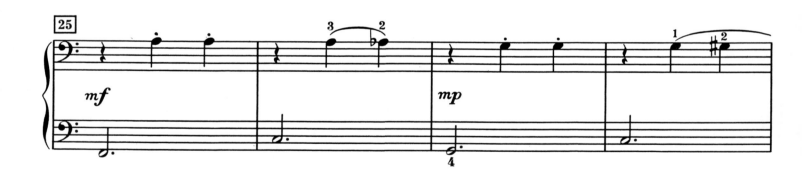

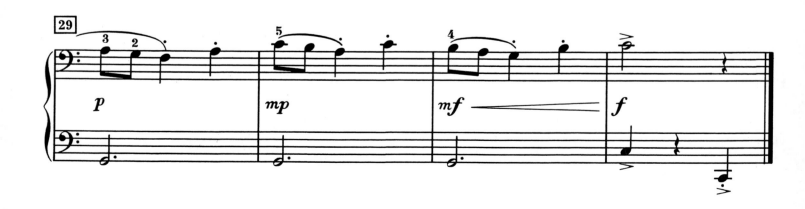

Bears on Wheels

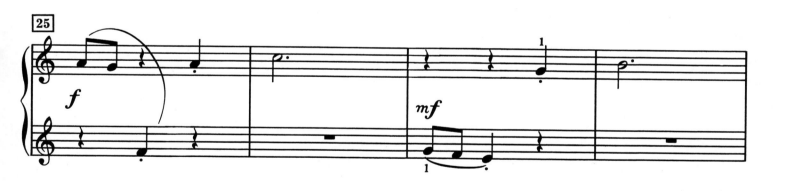

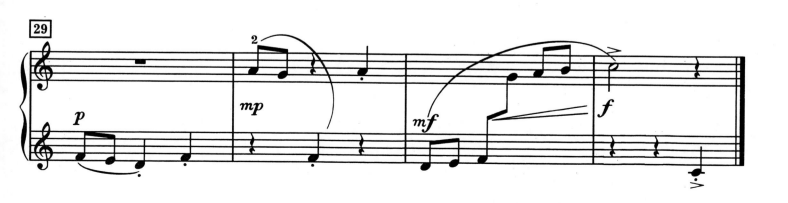

Babbling Bears

(Can You Bear It?)

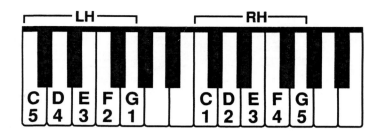

A lively conversation

Both hands 8va lower throughout

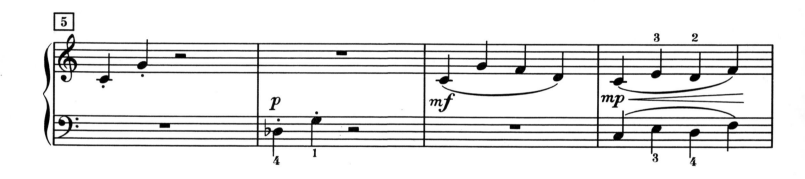

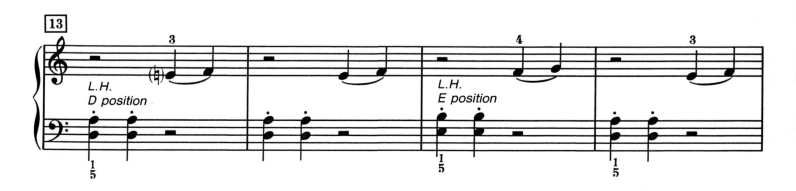

Babbling Bears
(Can You Bear It?)

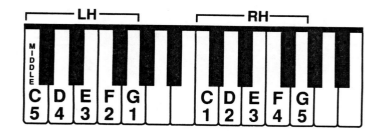

A lively conversation

Both hands 8va higher throughout

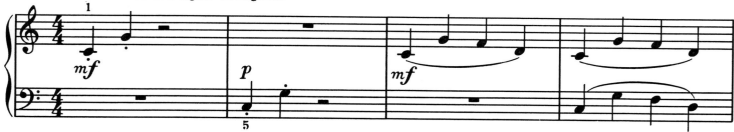

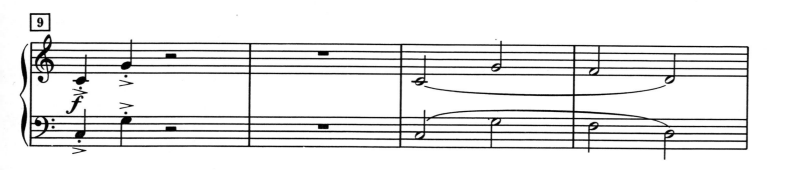

Babbling Bears

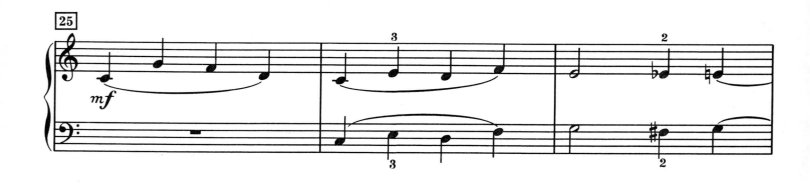

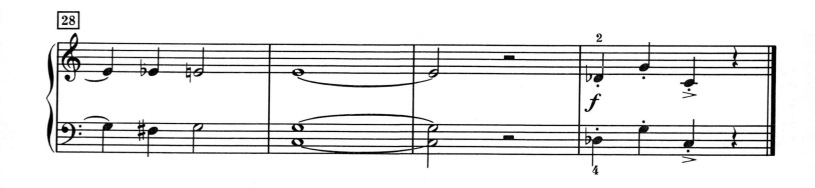

Babbling Bears

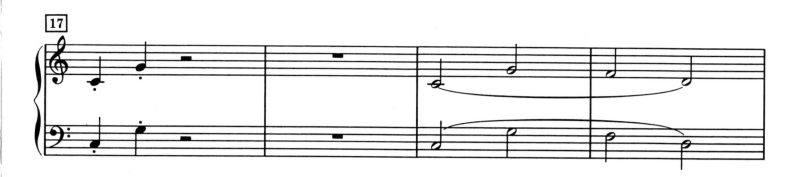

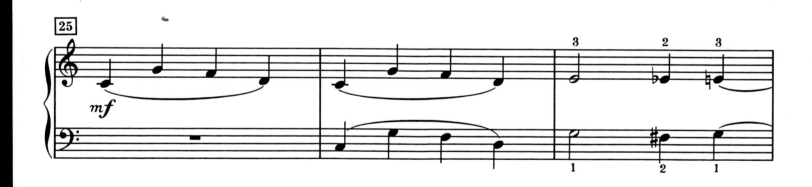

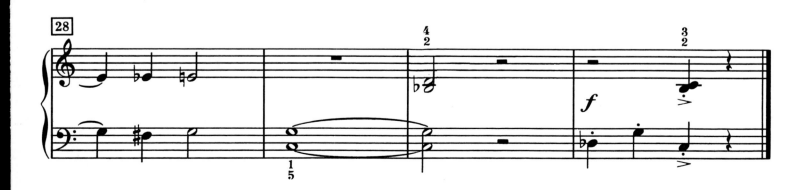

Bear Hug
(A Lullaby)

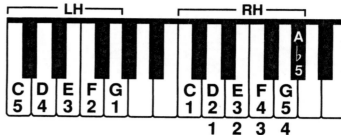

Beary lovingly

Both hands 8va lower throughout*

* Pedal may be used if desired (for example, measures 1-2, 3-4, etc.). In ms. 23-24, it is preferred.

Bear Hug
(A Lullaby)

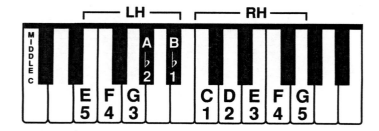

Beary lovingly

Both hands 8va higher throughout

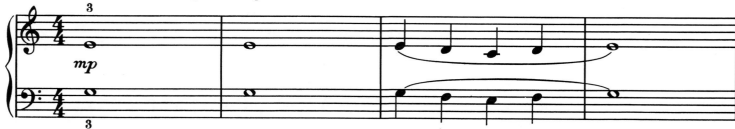

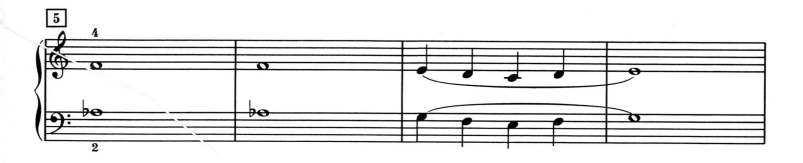

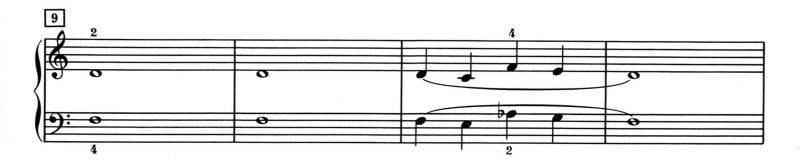

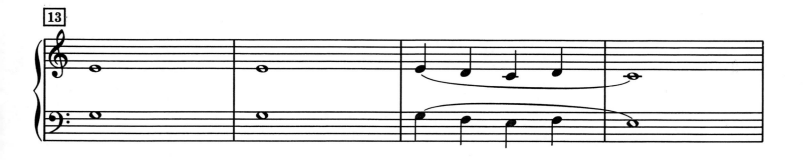

Bear Hug

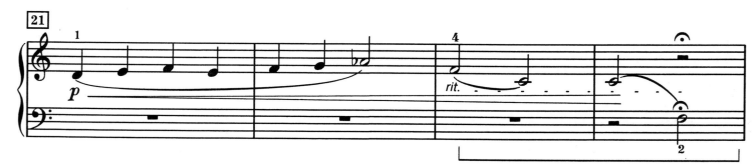

Bear Hug

Steps in the Forest
(Furward March!)

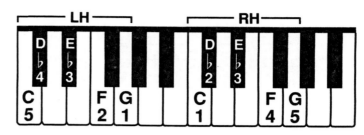

Pawmpously

Both hands 8va lower throughout

Steps in the Forest

(Furward March!)